SECOND EDITION

TOUCHSTONE

WORKBOOK 4B

T0139430

MICHAEL MCCARTHY
JEANNE MCCARTEN
HELEN SANDIFORD

CAMBRIDGE
UNIVERSITY PRESS

CAMBRIDGE
UNIVERSITY PRESS

University Printing House, Cambridge CB2 8BS, United Kingdom

One Liberty Plaza, 20th Floor, New York, NY 10006, USA

477 Williamstown Road, Port Melbourne, VIC 3207, Australia

314–321, 3rd Floor, Plot 3, Splendor Forum, Jasola District Centre, New Delhi – 110025, India

103 Penang Road, #05-06/07, Visioncrest Commercial, Singapore 238467

Cambridge University Press is part of the University of Cambridge.

It furthers the University's mission by disseminating knowledge in the pursuit of education, learning and research at the highest international levels of excellence.

www.cambridge.org
Information on this title: www.cambridge.org/9781107696020

© Cambridge University Press 2005, 2014

First published 2005
Second Edition 2014

20 19 18 17 16 15 14 13 12 11 10 9 8

Printed in Great Britain by CPI Group (UK) Ltd, Croydon CR0 4YY

A catalog record for this publication is available from the British Library.

ISBN 978-1-107-68043-2 Student's Book
ISBN 978-1-107-62430-6 Student's Book A
ISBN 978-1-107-63748-1 Student's Book B
ISBN 978-1-107-68275-7 Workbook
ISBN 978-1-107-62708-6 Workbook A
ISBN 978-1-107-69602-0 Workbook B
ISBN 978-1-107-66153-2 Full Contact
ISBN 978-1-107-67936-8 Full Contact A
ISBN 978-1-107-66763-1 Full Contact B
ISBN 978-1-107-68151-4 Teacher's Edition with Assessment Audio CD/CD-ROM
ISBN 978-1-107-61272-3 Class Audio CDs (4)

Additional resources for this publication at www.cambridge.org/touchstone2

Contents

Problem solving

Lesson A — Getting things done

1 Get someone else on the job!

Grammar | Read each sentence. Then circle the correct verbs to complete the sentences.

1. My sister never **gets** / (**has**) a mechanic check her oil. She just **gets** / **has** her brother to do it.

2. My boss always **gets** / **has** someone at the copy shop make his copies.

3. When my friend sold her small house, she **got** / **had** a famous architect design and build her a new one.

4. I hate doing the dishes, so I **get** / **have** my little sister to do them.

2 Get a professional.

Grammar | Complete the radio advertisements with the correct form of the verbs.

1. When your car is dirty, get a professional _to wash_ (wash) it at Jake's Car Wash. Cheap prices. Friendly service. Get your car _washed_ (wash) at Jake's today!

2. Have you always done your own decorating or gotten a friend _____ (do) it? This spring, why not have your home _____ (redecorate) by Paint Works? No job too big or too small.

3. Need a new image? Come to Alice's Salon to have your hair _____ (cut) by an expert. Get our stylists _____ (help) you choose the style that's right for you.

4. Don't pay a fortune to have your car _____ (repair). When your car breaks down, call Joe's Garage and get it _____ (fix) for less.

5. With your busy lifestyle, you don't have time for chores. From now on, get Helping Hands _____ (do) them for you. Whether you want to have the whole house _____ (clean) or just some shirts _____ (iron), we're here to help.

3 Get some advice online.

Grammar Jerry just moved to a new city. He posted these questions on an online forum. Complete the answers with the pairs of words in the box. Add appropriate pronouns.

get / clean	have / deliver	have / paint
✓ get / repair	have / fix	

Forum

Jerry85	My camera's making a funny noise. I can't afford a new one. Does anyone repair cameras these days?
StanP	You can _get it repaired_____ at Mick's Repairs. They're pretty cheap.
Jerry85	My TV's not working. Can someone recommend a good shop?
LilyRose	I like Gus's TV Shop. It won't cost a lot to _____ there.
Jerry85	Help! I need to find a really good dry cleaner's. I spilled spaghetti sauce all over my silk shirt last night.
JuanJ	When my clothes are stained, I always _____ at Main Street Cleaners. It's expensive, but they do a great job.
Jerry85	Where can I buy really fresh fruits and vegetables near Fry Street?
Hwatanabe	There's a health-food store on the corner of Fry and Middle Streets. You can also buy your groceries online and _____ .
Jerry85	My apartment needs painting. Does anyone know a professional painter?
Psmith89	It will cost a lot to _____ professionally. Could you paint it yourself?

4 About you

Grammar and vocabulary Answer the questions with true information.

1. What's something you usually pay to have someone do for you?
    _I usually pay to have someone fix my motorcycle._____

2. What's something you get a family member to do for you?
    _____

3. How much does it cost to get your hair cut?
    _____

4. What's something you would have done by a professional?
    _____

5. What's the last thing you had repaired?
    _____

6. If the screen on your laptop got damaged, would you get it fixed or buy a new laptop?
    _____

1 What's wrong?

Vocabulary Circle the best words to complete April's thoughts.

1. The mouse isn't working. I'll have to **recharge** / **fix** the battery.
2. I should really **tighten** / **upgrade** this software. I don't have the latest version.
3. Something's wrong with the monitor. I've tried **adjusting** / **replacing** the settings, but it's just not right.
4. Maybe I just need to **clean** / **recharge** the screen.
5. If it can't be fixed, I wonder if the store will **replace** / **adjust** it.

2 A fixer-upper

Grammar and vocabulary Look at the picture. Describe the problems. Write eight sentences with *need* + verb + *-ing* or *need* + passive infinitive. Use the verbs in the box.

adjust
clean
fix
paint
repair
replace
throw away
✓ tighten

1. *The lightbulb needs to be tightened.*
2. _____
3. _____
4. _____
5. _____
6. _____
7. _____
8. _____

3 Leaks and dents

Vocabulary | Complete the conversations with the words and phrases in the box.

dead	get a shock	making a funny noise	torn
✓dent	hole	slow	won't turn on
fall off	leaking	stain	
flickering	loose	stopped	

1. A What happened to your car? There's a big _____dent_____ in the door.
   And look, the oil is _____ .

   B Well, I was driving to school, and the car started _____ .
   So, I pulled over to the side of the road and hit a tree by accident.

2. A What happened? You're 15 minutes late.

   B Am I? My watch must be _____ . Uh-oh. It looks like it's _____ .

3. A Oh, no! The computer's not working. It's completely _____ .

   B You know, yesterday the screen kept _____ on and off.

   A Well, now it _____ at all. Maybe I should check the cables.

   B OK. Just be careful. You don't want to _____ .

4. A I had a horrible day. First, I spilled coffee on my new jeans.

   B Ooh. I bet that left a terrible _____ .

   A It did. Then, on the way home from work, I tripped and fell. Now my pants are stained, *and* they
   have a big _____ in them.

   B Well, _____ jeans are fashionable right now!

5. A Look at this old cabinet I found. I think I can fix it up nicely.

   B Really? All the knobs are _____ . And the legs – they all look like they're about to
   _____ . Are you sure you can fix it?

   A Oh, yeah. I repair furniture all the time.

4 About you

Grammar | Write true answers. Use *need* + verb + *-ing* or *need* + passive infinitive.

1. What's something in your home that needs cleaning?
   My kitchen always needs cleaning.
   _____

2. What's something in your home that needs to be tightened sometimes?
   _____

3. What's something in your home that sometimes needs to be adjusted?
   _____

4. What's something you own that needs to be recharged?
   _____

5. What's something you own that needs replacing?
   _____

1 Like it?

A Match each sentence with its shorter version.

1. Do you like it? _d_
2. I'm ready! _____
3. I'd love to! _____
4. Do you want me to help you? _____
5. Do you need some help moving it? _____
6. Do you want me to get it? _____
7. Do you want one? _____
8. Have you got any chips? _____
9. Are you ready? _____

a. Want me to help?
b. Ready?
c. Want one?
✓d. Like it?
e. Ready!
f. Got any chips?
g. Need some help moving it?
h. Want me to get it?
i. Love to!

B Complete the conversations with the shorter sentences from part A.

1. A Oh, that looks heavy. _Need some help moving it?_

   B No. I think I can carry it by myself. But thanks anyway.

2. A _____

   B Yes. I'm all ready to go.

   A Wow. That's a beautiful dress!

   B _____

   A Yeah, I really do!

3. A Gosh, I'm hungry. _____

   B No, but I have some cookies. _____

   A Sure. Thanks.

4. A Oh, I can't figure out how to use this new computer program.

   B _____

   A Oh, yeah. That would be great!

5. A Oh, there's the phone. I'm busy washing the dishes.

   B _____

   A Yes, please. Could you just take a message? Thanks.

6. A Are you hungry? Want to get some sushi?

   B _____

   A Great. Are you ready to go now?

   B Yeah. _____

2 Ooh!

Conversation strategies | **Circle the best word to begin each sentence.**

1. (**Ooh!**)/ **Ouch!** I see why it isn't working!

2. **Yuck! / Ow!** That hurt!

3. **Ugh! / Whoops!** I poured too much!

4. **Yuck! / Oops!** This tastes awful!

5. **Shoot! / Ouch!** I missed the bus.

6. **Uh-oh! / Ow!** The sink is leaking.

3 Scrambled conversations

Conversation strategies | **Number the lines of the conversations in the correct order.**

1. _____ OK, put it down. How does it look?

    _1_ Need some help moving the table?

    _____ Hmm. Don't like it there. Let's move it back.

    _____ Yes, please. It's heavy. I can't move it by myself.

    _____ Ready. OK. . . . Ooh! . . . It's heavy.

    _____ OK. Let's lift it together. Ready?

2. _____ How about that new horror movie – *Monster Girl*?

    _____ Love to. What movie do you want to see?

    _____ OK. What time is it playing?

    _____ Too bad! Want to go out for dessert instead?

    _____ Let me check. Shoot! We just missed the 7:00 show.

    _____ Want to go to the movies tonight?

1 Brainteasers

Reading | **A Read the puzzles. How many can you answer without looking at the solutions?**

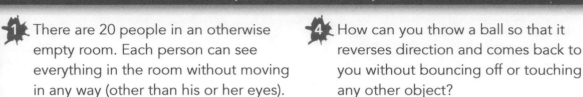

Here are some problems to solve,
JUST FOR FUN!

1 There are 20 people in an otherwise empty room. Each person can see everything in the room without moving in any way (other than his or her eyes). Where can you place an apple so that all but one person can see it?

2 A man was taking a walk outside when it started to rain. He didn't have an umbrella, and he wasn't wearing a hat. When he got home, his clothes were soaked, but not a single hair on his head got wet. How is this possible?

3 A painting hangs on the wall at a person's house. When the person is asked who is in the painting, the person replies, "I don't have a brother or a sister, but my mother's daughter is that man's mother." Who is the portrait of?

4 How can you throw a ball so that it reverses direction and comes back to you without bouncing off or touching any other object?

5 If it takes two men four hours to dig a hole, how much time does it take them to dig half a hole?

6 You are walking through a field, and you find something to eat. It doesn't have legs, and it doesn't have meat. You take it home and put it someplace warm. Three days later, it gets up and walks away. What is it?

7 Rearrange these letters into one long word: doornonegwl.

B Match each puzzle above with its solution.

a. "one long word" __7__
b. Throw it straight up in the air. _____
c. The man is bald. _____
d. An egg. _____

e. The owner's son. _____
f. On someone's head. _____
g. You can't dig half a hole! _____

C Find these words and expressions in the puzzles. Match them with their definitions.

1. (puzzle 1) but __c__
2. (puzzle 2) soaked _____
3. (puzzle 2) not a single _____
4. (puzzle 3) portrait _____
5. (puzzle 4) reverses direction _____
6. (puzzle 4) bouncing off _____

a. not one
b. hitting something and moving away quickly
✓c. except
d. a painting of a person
e. goes in the opposite direction
f. very wet

2 Interesting proposal

Writing **A** Read the proposal below. Circle the problem. Underline the solution and benefits.
Then put parentheses ( ) around how the solution will be implemented.

I find that there is sometimes a lack of understanding and respect between students and teachers.

In order to solve this problem, we should have a teacher–student swap day once a semester. On this day, students would be the teachers, and teachers would be the students. The reason for this is so that students and teachers can learn from the challenges the others face. This could benefit the school in several ways. First, students could see what teachers have to do to prepare for a class. Second, teachers could learn new ideas from students and how students learn best. Another advantage would be that students could find out if teaching is something they'd like to do as a career.

This could easily be put into practice. Each semester, every teacher would become a student and let two students take over the class – one in the morning and one in the afternoon. Students who are interested would volunteer to teach a subject they feel comfortable with. They would then be chosen at random.

B Write about a solution to a problem. Explain its benefits and how it can be implemented.
Use these ideas or your own.

- Too much litter in the city
- Not enough opportunities to practice English outside the classroom
- Ineffective public transportation

Unit 7 Progress chart

What can you do? Mark the boxes. ☑ = I can . . . ? = I need to review how to . . .	To review, go back to these pages in the Student's Book.
Grammar ☐ make sentences using causative *get* and *have*.	66 and 67
☐ use *need* + passive infinitive and *need* + verb + *-ing*.	68 and 69
Vocabulary ☐ use 5 new verbs to talk about fixing problems.	68
☐ use at least 10 new expressions to describe everyday problems.	69
Conversation strategies ☐ use "shorter sentences" in informal conversations.	70
☐ use at least 6 expressions for when things go wrong.	71
Writing ☐ present a solution to a problem.	73

1 It's not nice to sulk.

Vocabulary | **What are these people doing? Write sentences using the words and expressions in the box.**

| hang up | hug | laugh out loud | lose his temper | ✓sulk | yell |

1. *He's sulking.*   2. _____   3. _____

4. _____   5. _____   6. _____

2 I wouldn't have yelled at him.

Grammar and vocabulary | **Read each comment. Say what you would have done and what you wouldn't have done. Use the ideas in Exercise 1, or add your own.**

1. "Last night, a guy cut in line and bought the last two tickets for the movie I wanted to see!"
   I would have been annoyed. I wouldn't have yelled at him, though.

2. "Yesterday, my aunt gave me $100 for my birthday."
   _____

3. "My best friend told me a really funny joke in the middle of science class."
   _____

4. "Last week, I failed my math exam."
   _____

5. "My little brother accidentally deleted all the phone numbers from my smartphone."
   _____

3 What would you have done?

Grammar **A** Complete the conversations with past modal verbs. Use the words given.

1. Rita   My uncle gave me this painting last year. It's not really my taste.

    Leah   Hmm. Well, you _could have taken_ (could / take) it back to the store.

    Rita   I _____ (could not / do) that. He painted it himself.

            And anyway, I _____ (would not / want) to upset him.

            He's such a nice guy.

    Leah   Well, I guess the only thing you _____ (could / do) was

            smile and say thank you.

    Rita   That's exactly what I did. I _____ (would not / say) anything

            else. Though I guess I _____ (should / sound) a little more

            enthusiastic.

2. Luz   You know, I was upset that Cora didn't come to my party last month.

    Jon   Yeah, I think I _____ (would / be) upset, too.

    Luz   I was, but I guess I _____ (should / call) her to see if she

           was coming.

    Jon   Maybe. But she still _____ (could / contact) you. Although

           maybe she was sick and couldn't call.

    Luz   Yeah, I didn't think about that. But she _____ (should / get) her

           mother to call and tell me. That's what I _____ (would / do).

    Jon   Yeah, but you never know. Why don't you call and find out what happened?

B Write questions with past modals that Rita and Luz could have asked in the conversations in part A. Then write your own answers.

Questions   **Answers**

Conversation 1

1. What else / I / say ?

    What else could I have said?   _____

2. How / you / react ?

    _____   _____

3. you / hang / it up ?

    _____   _____

Conversation 2

4. you / feel / angry ?

    _____   _____

5. you / call her ?

    _____   _____

6. What / Cora / do ?

    _____   _____

1 What's your personality?

Vocabulary | Read what each person says about himself or herself. Write three words that best describe each person.

aggressive	decisive	flexible	honest	jealous	sensitive
confident	determined	✓happy	impulsive	realistic	sympathetic

1. I enjoy life. I'm pretty easygoing. If my friends want to do something, I'll usually go along with their plans, unless they're really crazy. I know what I'm capable and not capable of.

   <u> *happy* </u>   _____   _____

2. My friends often call me when something is worrying them. They say I'm a good listener, and I always tell them the truth. I don't like to see my friends upset or depressed.

   _____   _____   _____

3. I'm a pretty motivated person. I always know what I want. Once I decide to do something, I do it. I always try my hardest to achieve my goals.

   _____   _____   _____

4. What are my worst qualities? Well, I always want things that other people have. I sometimes lose my temper in stores and can shout if I don't get what I want. I guess I often do things without thinking about the consequences.

   _____   _____   _____

2 Positive or negative?

Vocabulary | Which words have a positive meaning for you, and which ones have a negative meaning? Complete the chart with the words in the box.

aggression	determination	happiness	motivation	sensitivity
anger	flexibility	hate	realism	shame
✓confidence	grief	honesty	sadness	sulking
depression	guilt	jealousy	self-discipline	sympathy

Positive		Negative	
confidence			

3 She must have!

Grammar | Rewrite the sentences in parentheses using past modal verbs. Use the modal verbs given.

1. A There's no answer. (must) *She must have left by now.*
   (I bet she left by now.)

   B Do you think she's coming by bus?

   A Um, I don't know. (may) _____
   (Maybe she decided to drive.)

   B I don't think so. Her car broke down. It was in the garage last night.
   (could not) _____
   (It's not possible she got it back yet.)

2. A Did I tell you someone robbed Dana last week and stole her purse?

   B How awful! (must) _____
   (I bet she was scared.)

   A Well, she was scared at first. The funny thing was, she knew the thief.
   She went to school with him! But Dana looks really different now.
   (might not) _____
   (So it's possible he didn't recognize her.)

   B Did she tell him that she knew him?

   A (may) _____ I don't really know.
   (Maybe she told him.)

   B Well, I hope she reported him to the police!

4 About you

Grammar | Read each situation. Use past modals to complete the sentences with possible reasons why these situations happened.

1. Your roommate overslept and missed an important meeting at work.
   She could *have stayed up too late the night before* .
   She might *not have set her alarm* .

2. Your best friend hasn't called you in a week.
   He / She may _____ .
   He / She couldn't _____ .

3. Your grandparents forgot your birthday.
   They may not _____ .
   They might _____ .

4. Your sister can't find her favorite earrings.
   She must _____ .
   She could _____ .

1 Rude behavior

Conversation strategies | **Complete the conversation with the expressions in the box.**

> I had a similar thing happen to me,   That reminds me of the time
> ✓ I had that happen to me   That's like
> That happened to my friend Nancy,   Speaking of

A She just cut in line! It drives me crazy when people do that.

B _I had that happen to me_ last week. Same thing. This woman in the store just pushed her cart right in front of me. I looked at her, and she was like, "Too bad." She was so rude.

A Don't you hate that? _____ people who push right past you in the street. You know, when it's busy. It can really hurt.

B I know. _____ a guy walked right into me on Main Street. He never even apologized.

A Wasn't he looking?

B I guess not. Has that ever happened to you – someone walking directly into you?

A Well, not quite. I mean, _____ but with a door – and I walked into *it*!

B No way! _____ too. She walked into a glass door and knocked herself out! She was in a hurry and wasn't looking where she was going.

A _____ being in a hurry, I have to get going myself. I'll see you tomorrow!

2 Like, what?

Conversation strategies | **Read the sentences. Which meaning of *like* is used? Write the letter.**

> a. to give an example   d. to report what someone said
> b. to highlight something   ✓ e. to say *approximately*
> c. to say something is similar

1. I've known Giovanni for like ten years. __*e*__

2. My mom asked me to look for her car keys, and I was like, "Again!?" _____

3. I'm always like so tired in the morning, and it's so hard to get out of bed. _____

4. I'm just like my father – we're both tall, athletic, and easygoing. _____

5. My little sister loves TV. Like, she's always watching cartoons or game shows. _____

6. I've been studying for like weeks so that I do well on my final exams. _____

7. I wanted to leave work early tonight, but my boss was like, "You can't leave until you finish your report." _____

8. I'm always forgetting things. Like, I went to the supermarket the other day, and I forgot what I was supposed to buy! _____

3 I was like, "I'm sorry."

Conversation strategies | **What does each speaker say next? Write the letter.**

1. One of my friends is really sensitive. _d_
2. My sister forgot to call me again. _____
3. My aunt is pretty old. _____
4. My mom is like really impulsive. _____
5. My friend is very motivated, just like me. _____
6. A co-worker got so upset with me. _____

a. She like never remembers!
b. She's like 80 years old!
c. We're both determined to do well in school.
✓d. Like, she's always crying about nothing.
e. I was like, "I'm sorry. I didn't realize."
f. Like, she does things without thinking.

4 Like, I had a similar experience!

Conversation strategies | **Respond to each statement and describe a similar experience. Use the expressions in the box. Can you add a sentence using *like* with one of the meanings in Exercise 2 on page 62?**

I had that happen to me.
That happened to me.
I had a similar experience.
That reminds me (of) . . .
That's like . . .
Speaking of . . . ,

1. I went to a new hairdresser, and the guy did a terrible job with my hair. I looked ridiculous.

   I had a similar experience at the hairdresser last year. I asked for like curly hair, and when I left, I looked terrible.

2. A guy called last night while I was eating dinner. He wanted me to send money to a charity or something.

   _____
   _____
   _____

3. I was supposed to meet a friend at the movies last night, but she never showed up.

   _____
   _____
   _____

4. Last night I was at this restaurant, and a man at a table near me talked on his cell phone the whole time.

   _____
   _____
   _____

5. I have a friend who always interrupts me when I tell a story. It drives me crazy.

   _____
   _____
   _____

1 I'm peeved!

Reading | **A Read the blogs. What do the two stories have in common?**

☐ The problems were solved by yelling at the person.   ☐ The problems weren't solved.

☐ Both bloggers yelled at someone.   ☐ Both bloggers took action to solve the problems.

○ ○ ○   Pet Peeves

Pet Peeves

We asked our bloggers to write in with their pet peeves and tell us how they deal with the things that annoy them the most.

MARGARET, 32, OTTAWA If there's one thing that upsets me, it's people who throw their trash on the street. It really makes me angry when I see people toss their food wrappers and empty soda cans on the sidewalk. They should be ashamed of themselves, but people don't seem to feel at all guilty about it. I see it happen all the time, and afterward I always say to myself, "I should have said something." So finally I did.

I was walking down my block the other day, and this guy was coming toward me, and he threw his cup right into my neighbor's garden! What nerve! Now, I could have ignored it and carried on walking without saying a thing – as I usually do – but I know I would have regretted it. I was determined to do something this time because it was right there in my neighborhood! So I yelled at him. I probably shouldn't have done that, but I kind of lost my temper! I said, "You know, Mrs. Tweedy worked really hard on that garden, and you just threw your trash in it. And there's a garbage can right on the corner!" He seemed pretty embarrassed and said, "You're right. I'm sorry." Then he went and got his cup. I was really surprised, but I'm glad it turned out like that – he could have gotten mad at me or turned aggressive or something. Anyway, I felt great for the rest of the day, and in the future, I'll always stop and tell people to pick up their trash – though I probably won't yell like that!

ZACH, 21, MIAMI I can't stand it when people send me links to silly video clips. I'm talking about those cat videos or clips of blurry concert footage. It's so time-consuming because you feel obliged to watch them and send a comment back. Sometimes it makes you kind of question your friends' tastes and why they think these videos are funny. They just post links on everybody's social networking pages without thinking. I mean, sometimes I see something funny and post it on someone's wall, but I always include a personal comment. And I don't send things to everybody I'm friends with online.

I have this friend who used to post links on my wall all the time – like at least once a day. Some of them were funny, but some of them were kind of weird. In the end, I sent her a private message asking her – in a very nice way – to stop. She apologized and stopped. She said she sympathized because someone was sending her game requests up to four times a day, so she knew how annoying it could be. I thought, "So why do it, then?"

B Find these words and phrases in the blogs. Match them with their definitions.

1. pet peeves *f*

2. toss _____

3. What nerve! _____

4. carried on _____

5. time-consuming _____

6. obliged _____

a. continued

b. How rude!

c. forced

d. taking a lot of time

e. throw

✓ f. frustrations; irritations

C Read the blogs again. Then answer the questions.

1. What does Margaret usually do when she sees people throw trash on the street? _____

_____

2. Why did she decide to respond differently this time? _____

3. What does she think she should have done differently? _____

4. Why doesn't Zach like getting links from his friends? _____

5. Why did Zach's friend finally sympathize with him? _____

2 Apologies

Writing **A** Read the apology letter. Fill in the blanks with the expressions in the box.

I feel I should apologize for	I just hope	I promise not to	it was my fault entirely

Dear Mr. Feaster,

_____ letting my dog run in your garden the other day. I was talking on my cell phone, and I didn't notice he was digging up your flowers. I should have paid more attention. I know _____ . _____ let my dog into your garden again. _____ that you can accept my apology.

Sincerely,
Janice Brown

B Think of something you've done in the past and write a note of apology.

_____
_____
_____

Unit 8 Progress chart

What can you do? Mark the boxes. ✓ = I can . . . ? = I need to review how to . . .	To review, go back to these pages in the Student's Book.
Grammar ☐ use past modals to talk hypothetically about the past.	76 and 77
☐ use past modals to speculate about the past.	79
Vocabulary ☐ use at least 6 words and expressions to discuss behavior.	76 and 77
☐ use 15 new words to talk about emotions and personality.	78
Conversation strategies ☐ use expressions like *Speaking of* and *That's like* to share my experiences.	80
☐ use *like* in different ways.	81
Writing ☐ use expressions to apologize.	83

Material world

Lesson A / Possessions

1 Things and stuff

Vocabulary | **A** Complete the questions with the words and expressions in the box.

accumulated	materialistic	part with
goals	✓ own	possessions

1. Do you ____own____ a lot of valuable things?
2. How attached are you to the things you own –
   especially your most valuable _____ ?
3. What things do you find hard to throw away
   or _____ ?
4. What kinds of objects have you collected or
   _____ over time?
5. What are your main aims or _____
   for this coming year?
6. How _____ are you?

B Answer the questions from part A with your own information.

1. *I don't own anything of great value, really, but I want to start collecting art.*
   I have a lot of personal items, like clothes and books, though.

2. _____

   _____

3. _____

   _____

4. _____

   _____

5. _____

   _____

6. _____

   _____

2 What did they say?

Grammar and vocabulary | Read the statements. Then complete the sentences to report what the people said.

1. "I think I'll clean out my closets soon."
   My sister said that she ____thought____ she _'d clean out_ her closets soon.

2. "I've been saving money to buy a new car."
   My friend said that he _____ money to buy a new car.

3. "I haven't found a new dress for the wedding yet."
   My mom said that she _____ a new dress for the wedding yet.

4. "I can't part with my favorite jeans, even though they're torn."
   My cousin said he _____ his favorite jeans, even though they _____ torn.

5. "My goal is to pay off my credit card debt by next year."
   My older brother said that his goal _____ to pay off his credit card debt by next year.

6. "I'm always buying shoes. I think I have 30 pairs."
   My dad said that he _____ shoes and that he _____ he _____ 30 pairs.

7. "I won't ever throw out my favorite photographs."
   My grandma said that she _____ her favorite photographs.

8. "My parents bought me a beautiful pearl necklace."
   My aunt said that her parents _____ her a beautiful pearl necklace.

3 Her mother's a millionaire.

Grammar | Rewrite the direct speech as reported speech.

Mel Did you have a good time on your date with Ariel last week?
I saw her at a café yesterday, and she said _she'd enjoyed it a lot_____ .
("I enjoyed it a lot.")

Eric Yeah, it was fine. The only thing was I had to pay for everything.
Ariel said _____ . Then she said
("I'm broke.")

that _____ .
("I've been spending too much lately.")

Mel So you paid for the movies and dinner, too?

Eric Yes. She said _____ .
("I can't afford to buy the tickets.")

Mel Are you going to see her again?

Eric I don't know. She told me _____
("I'm going away for a week.")

and that _____ .
("I'll call you when I get back.")

Mel I hope she doesn't get back before your next paycheck! Where's she going anyway?

Eric Well, she said _____ .
("It's a surprise.")

Her mother was sending her someplace exotic.

Mel Yeah. She once told me _____ .
("My mother's a millionaire.")

1 Money matters

Vocabulary Circle the correct words to complete each money expression.

1. get into   a. money   (b.) debt   c. payment
2. pay good   a. account   b. budget   c. interest
3. pay in   a. cash   b. check   c. credit card
4. invest   a. account   b. money   c. debt
5. keep track   a. off   b. aside   c. of
6. charge to   a. a credit card   b. a loan   c. a budget
7. set _____ money   a. away   b. aside   c. off
8. pay _____ a loan   a. off   b. away   c. aside
9. take out   a. an interest   b. a debt   c. a loan

2 Smart money tips

Vocabulary Complete the sentences and puzzle below with the words in the box.

away	bills	✓charge	debt	income	monthly	out	savings	stocks

1. Don't __charge__ too much to your credit card, unless you can pay it off in full every month.
2. It's important to pay your _____ on time. You shouldn't let them pile up.
3. Sticking to a _____ budget can save you money.
4. Many people take _____ loans to pay for cars or homes.
5. Try to put _____ some money every month for emergencies.
6. Shop around for a _____ account that pays good interest.
7. People sometimes take several jobs to increase their _____ .
8. You can invest in a company by buying _____ .
9. It's important to get out of _____ to avoid paying large sums of interest.

1. _c_ _h_ _a_ _r_ _g_ _e_
2. ___ ___ ___ ___ ___
3. ___ ___ ___ ___ ___ ___ ___
4. ___ ___ ___
5. ___ ___ ___ ___
6. ___ ___ ___ ___ ___ ___ ___
7. ___ ___ ___ ___ ___ ___
8. ___ ___ ___ ___ ___ ___
9. ___ ___ ___

When children do chores around the house, they often get an _____ .

3 He asked me . . .

Grammar | **Imagine you met with a financial adviser to talk about your spending habits. Read the financial adviser's questions. Then complete the reported questions.**

1. "How much money do you save each month?"

   He asked me *how much money I saved* each month.

2. "Do you have any credit card or other debt?"

   He wanted to know _____ any credit card or other debt.

3. "Can you stick to a monthly budget?"

   He wanted to know _____ a monthly budget.

4. "How many times have you taken money out of your savings account this month?"

   He asked _____ money out of my savings account this month.

5. "What do you spend most of your money on?"

   He wanted to know _____ most of my money on.

6. "Have you taken out a loan recently?"

   He asked me _____ a loan recently.

4 Where did the money go?

Grammar | **Read what Amy says and the questions her family asks her. Then change the direct questions into reported questions by completing the sentences below.**

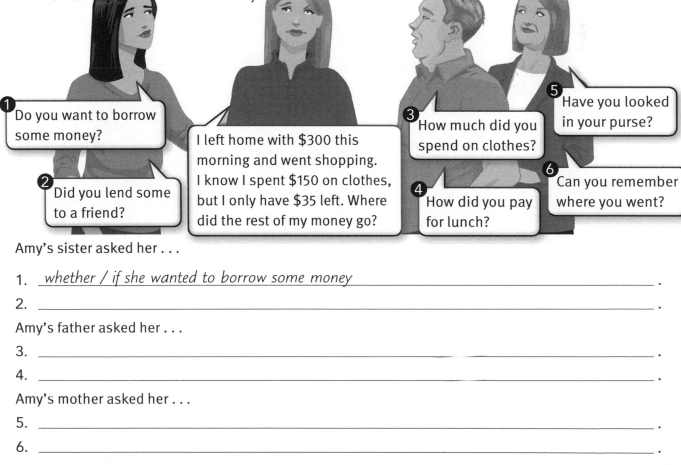

Sister   Amy   Father   Mother

❶ Do you want to borrow some money?

❷ Did you lend some to a friend?

I left home with $300 this morning and went shopping. I know I spent $150 on clothes, but I only have $35 left. Where did the rest of my money go?

❸ How much did you spend on clothes?

❹ How did you pay for lunch?

❺ Have you looked in your purse?

❻ Can you remember where you went?

Amy's sister asked her . . .

1. *whether / if she wanted to borrow some money* _____.

2. _____.

Amy's father asked her . . .

3. _____.

4. _____.

Amy's mother asked her . . .

5. _____.

6. _____.

1 What was she telling you?

Conversation
strategies
Read these reports of conversations. Rewrite the underlined sentences as reported speech using past continuous reporting verbs.

I was talking with my neighbor yesterday. (1) She told me about her son. He's planning to do some community work for a few years. (2) She said it doesn't pay much. But he thinks it'll be a good experience anyway.

(3) A co-worker of mine told me our boss just won the lottery. I can't believe it! She never buys lottery tickets! But she bought one on impulse, and she won! (4) My co-worker said she won $5,000. So, hopefully, she'll buy us lunch today.

(5) My friend told me she needs a new car. Her car is always breaking down, and she's been late to work five times this month. (6) She said that she might lose her job if she's late again.

I was talking to my brother on the phone last night. (7) I told him what to do while I'm on vacation. So, he's going to feed my cat and water my plants. And I told him where things were.

1. *She was telling me about her son.*

2. _____

3. _____

4. _____

5. _____

6. _____

7. _____

2 Who told you?

Conversation strategies Complete the conversations with the expressions in the boxes.

✓evidently	I've heard	told me

1. A Wow! We have so much stuff in our closets. There's no more room.

   B I know. ___Evidently___ , there's a new TV show where this woman helps you get rid of all the stuff you don't want anymore.

   A Really?

   B Yeah, Seth _____ about it. They take everything you own and put it outside your house. You have to sell or throw away more than half of it!

   A Oh, yeah. _____ it's a fun show.

according to the report	they say	was saying

2. A Did you hear the news about interest rates?

   B Yeah, I did. _____ on TV last night, they're going up – again!

   A That's right. _____ we'll have to pay around 25% on our credit cards.

   B I know. Isn't that terrible?

   A Yeah. But, as my friend _____ , it might stop us from spending so much.

apparently	he was telling me	I was told

3. A Did you get tickets for the school concert tonight?

   B It's tonight? _____ it was next week.

   A No, it's tonight. _____ , it's going to be a great show. I talked to Henry earlier today, and _____ it's already sold out.

   B Oh, no. I guess I'm not going, then.

3 About you

Conversation strategies Answer the questions with true information. Use past continuous reporting verbs and expressions from Exercise 2.

1. What's an interesting TV show you've heard about recently?

   _____

2. What's something you learned from the news?

   _____

3. What's some good or bad news someone just told you this week?

   _____

1 Books – pass them on!

Reading **A** Read the article. What do book swappers do with their books?

☐ sell them to charities
☐ share them with fellow readers
☐ add them to wish lists

The Web Is Your Library!

What do you do when you've finished reading a book? Do you put it back on your bookshelf and forget about it, or do you pass it on to other readers through book swapping – exchanging books with friends, colleagues, book groups, or members of online book-swapping sites? Book swapping solves a number of problems for people who still love to read print books, such as how to find space to store their books and how not to spend lots of money purchasing new ones.

Over the years, dozens of book-swapping sites have popped up on the Internet. Each site has its own rules and regulations, but the basic idea is the same. Members register the books they wish to swap on the site. Other members browse through the postings and then make contact if they are interested in a particular book. The book is then mailed by the person who posted it. Once the book is mailed, the person who posted it earns points, which then allows him or her to acquire a book from another online member.

Some online book-swapping sites let members keep a wish list of books they'd like to acquire. When one of the books on a member's wish list is posted on the website, that member will receive a message generated by the website saying who the book can be acquired from. Another feature of many book-swapping sites is the ability to donate your books to a charity. Donating books earns the same number of points as swapping with another member.

If you're not keen on using the Internet as a means of obtaining cheap books, second-hand bookstores and public libraries often offer book-swapping services. Or, if you prefer to know where your books come from, you can also set up a book swap in your own community.

B Read the article again. Then read the sentences below. Write *T* (true) or *F* (false) for each sentence. Then correct the false sentences.

1. Book swapping ~~creates~~ *solves* a number of problems for book lovers. _F_

2. All book-swapping sites have the same basic rules. _____

3. The person who requests a book on a book-swapping site earns points. _____

4. When a book on your wish list is posted, the person who posts it will contact you. _____

5. You earn the same number of points for a book when you donate it to a charity. _____

6. There are book-swapping schemes in some public libraries. _____

2 So many books

A Read the article about a book lover. Fill in the blanks with the expressions in the box.

she added   she concluded   ✓she explained   she recalled

Eunjoo Park has more than 5,000 books in her one-bedroom apartment. "I can't live without my books," _she explained_ . Her living room and bedroom are filled with bookshelves, and she is always buying more shelves. "It's better to buy more shelves than get rid of any books," _____ .

"Once, I decided to sell some books in a street sale," _____ . "When a woman came by and tried to buy a book, I couldn't sell it to her! I took my books back inside and put them away."

Now she knows better. "I just refuse to get rid of my books," she told me. "There seems to be only one solution – I just have to get a bigger apartment," _____ .

B Write an article about someone you know. Use reporting verbs to tell the person's story. Use an idea below or one of your own.

Someone who . . .

- collects something.
- often sells his or her things.
- is materialistic.

Unit 9 Progress chart

What can you do? Mark the boxes. ✓ = I can . . . ? = I need to review how to . . .	To review, go back to these pages in the Student's Book.
■ report things that people said.	86 and 87
■ report questions that people asked.	89
■ use 25 new expressions about possessions and money.	86, 87, 88, and 89
■ use past continuous reporting verbs to tell about a conversation.	90
■ use expressions like *They say*, *I've heard*, and *Evidently*.	91
■ use different reporting verbs to quote other people.	93

Grammar

Vocabulary

Conversation strategies

Writing

1 Kelly Clarkson's rise to fame

Grammar | **Read the information about pop star Kelly Clarkson. Then complete the sentences below using the past perfect and past modals.**

Kelly Clarkson was chosen from among hundreds of competitors to win *American Idol*, a TV talent show that lets viewers vote on the winner. Since winning, she has recorded a number of top-selling "hits" and has become a household name. Yet, her rise to fame came somewhat unexpectedly, as she had always dreamed of being a marine biologist.

1. If Kelly _had followed_ (follow) her career dream, she _might have become_ (might become) a marine biologist.

2. If a music teacher _____ (not hear) Kelly singing in the hall of her middle school, she _____ (not join) the school chorus.

3. If Kelly _____ (not learn) to sing classically in her school chorus, she _____ (might not be able) to use her voice in so many different ways.

4. If Kelly's friend _____ (not tell) her about *American Idol*, Kelly _____ (not try out) for the show.

5. If Kelly _____ (receive) 47% and not 57% of the final vote on *American Idol*, she _____ (not win) the competition.

2 More pop idols

Grammar | **Complete the interviews with the runners-up of a TV talent competition with the past perfect or past modal form of the verbs given. Sometimes more than one answer is possible.**

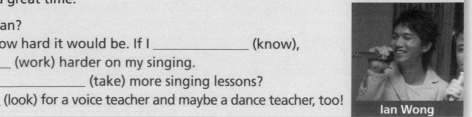

a Pop magazine EXCLUSIVE   THE POP ARTISTS YOU VOTED FOR!

THE RUNNERS-UP

PM   Why do you think you came in second, Beth?
Beth I definitely chose the wrong song. The judges didn't like it at all.
PM   So, if you _____ (not sing) that song, _____ you _____ (win), do you think?
Beth Who knows? I _____ (have) a better chance. But it doesn't really matter because I had a great time.

Beth Simon

PM   How are you feeling, Ian?
Ian   Well, I didn't realize how hard it would be. If I _____ (know), maybe I _____ (work) harder on my singing.
PM   _____ you _____ (take) more singing lessons?
Ian   Yeah, I _____ (look) for a voice teacher and maybe a dance teacher, too!

Ian Wong

3 She might have become a famous ballerina.

Grammar | **Complete each story with your own ideas. Use past modals.**

1. Emma was a top student in high school and in her dance classes. But then she dropped out of dance class to focus on her schoolwork. She then went on to study at Harvard University. If Emma hadn't stopped taking dance classes, *she might have / could have become a famous ballerina*
   or *she wouldn't have gone to Harvard* .

2. Maemi always wanted to be a doctor, but on her 13th birthday, her parents gave her a camera. That was the start of her interest in photography, and she later became a professional photographer. If Maemi hadn't gotten a camera for her birthday,

   _____ .

3. Stephanie loved to build things when she was younger. She even helped her father design an addition to their house. But when she was in high school, she was spotted by a modeling agency and became a model. She always says that _____ if she hadn't become a model.

4. Martin loved farming, but he had no interest in cooking. His grandmother nevertheless made him help her cook dinner every Sunday. Martin just opened his second organic restaurant. If his grandmother hadn't taught him how to cook,

   _____ .

5. Hao-xing, a trombone player, was taking part in a competition. As he stepped on stage, he noticed a beautiful woman in the front row of the audience. While he was playing his piece, he became distracted by the woman. He forgot the music and didn't win the competition. If he hadn't seen the woman, _____ .

4 About you

Grammar | **Complete the sentences with past modals and your own ideas.**

1. If I had left school at the age of 16, *I might not have met the teacher who inspired me the most* .
2. If I hadn't taken English, _____ .
3. _____ if I hadn't worked so hard.
4. If I had been born into a famous family, _____ .
5. _____ if I had practiced more.
6. If my parents hadn't _____, _____ .

1 Making headlines

Vocabulary | Complete the magazine article with the expressions in the box.

bad press	in the headlines
drop out of sight	in the right place
go downhill	made headlines
got discovered	take off
have connections	✓ up-and-coming

LUCKY STAR

Up-and-coming movie star Gianna LaRose was seen having lunch with her boyfriend of two years, Rich Marsh, in Los Angeles earlier this week. The couple seemed relaxed and happy, even after the _____ their relationship has gotten recently. Ms. LaRose denied rumors of a split and happily signed autographs for her fans.

After losing last year's Best Breakthrough Performance Award, many people thought LaRose's career could only _____ , but just the opposite has happened. Ms. LaRose _____ recently when she was offered the lead role in director Rick Callahan's new blockbuster. This young actress has everything going for her. It's unlikely she will _____ anytime soon. Her career is just getting started and is sure to _____ .

Ms. LaRose _____ five years ago while working at a movie theater. Talent agent Erica Menken saw LaRose and thought she had "star qualities." The rest is history, as they say. Ms. LaRose says she was lucky to meet Ms. Menken. She was studying to be an actress, but she didn't _____ in the movie industry. "Meeting Erica was an example of being _____ at the right time," Ms. LaRose said.

Expect to see Ms. LaRose's name _____ for a long time.

2 A movie date

Grammar | Complete the sentences below with the tag questions in the box.

1. It's great to go out and see a movie, _isn't it_____ ?
2. We're not going to be late for the movie, _____ ?
3. You haven't seen this movie yet, _____ ?
4. You liked the movie, _____ ?
5. It was interesting, _____ ?
6. That actor has been in a lot of movies, _____ ?

are we
didn't you
hasn't he
have you
✓ isn't it
wasn't it

3 Stars among us

Grammar | Complete the conversations with tag questions.

1. A Ben Affleck gives a lot of money to charity, _doesn't he_ ?

   B I didn't know that. You don't see it in the press very much,
      _____ ?

   A No, but then, people often do charitable things quietly,
      _____ ?

   B Maybe. But it's great to see someone who's so wealthy give money
      to good causes, _____ ?

   A Sure, but I wish someone would give some to me!

2. A Oh, my goodness. That isn't Taylor Swift, _____ ?

   B I don't think so. She doesn't hang out at this coffee shop,
      _____ ?

   A I don't know. I think it's her. She just let that girl take a picture of her,
      _____ ?

   B Hmm. It does kind of look like her, _____ ?

   A See, I was right, _____ ? Come on. Let's go over and
      take her picture, too!

4 Tell us about yourself.

Grammar | **Imagine you are going to interview actor Reese Witherspoon. Write tag questions you can ask her to check the following facts.**

Facts	Questions
1. raised in Nashville, Tennessee	*You were raised in Tennessee, weren't you?*
2. started acting at the age of seven	
3. first major role was in *The Man in the Moon*	
4. appeared in over 25 movies by the age of 30	
5. has produced several movies	
6. married to a talent agent	
7. has three children	

Good question!

1 Comic advice

Conversation strategies **Complete the conversation with tag questions.**

Tina Hey, Max. How was the comedy workshop you went to last week?

Max Great. I'd like to be a comedian someday, but I'm not sure I'm ready.

Tina Well, you could take another comedy workshop, _couldn't you_ ?

Max Yeah. . . . There's another one next month.

Tina Sounds good. You just need to call and sign up, _____ ?

Max Yeah. I wonder how all the famous comedians on TV got started.

Tina It would help to read some books about them, _____ ?

Max I guess. I'll look online tonight. You know, the hardest thing is writing new and original jokes.

Tina Well, you could look for some books on joke writing, too, _____ ?

Max Yeah. I mean, I learned a little bit about it in the workshop, but you never can tell what people will find funny.

Tina It would be a good idea to call some of the local comedy clubs, _____ ? And ask them if you could try out some of your jokes. They always need people to perform, _____ ? I'm sure the club owners could give you some advice, too. I mean, you need all the help you can get, _____ ?

Max Hey, that's not funny!

2 What's your advice?

Conversation strategies **Your friend is having a lot of bad luck lately. Read each situation, and give your best advice and encouragement using tag questions.**

1. I didn't do well on the last English test. I'm worried about my final grade.
   I'm sure you could ask to take the test again, couldn't you?

2. I want to practice my English, but I don't know any English-speaking people.
   _____

3. I got in a horrible fight with my best friend. I don't know what to do.
   _____

4. I've gained some weight over the holidays. I don't fit into my jeans!
   _____

5. I forgot my boyfriend's birthday and never got him a present.
   _____

6. I lost my mother's necklace. What am I going to do?
   _____

3 That's a good question.

Conversation strategies | **Match each question with the best response.**

1. What's the hardest thing about being famous? _b_

2. What do you plan to do next in your career? _____

3. Who inspires you in your work? _____

4. Do you consider yourself a role model? _____

5. What would you do if you weren't an actor? _____

a. That's a good question. I think I'd like to do some roles in theater.

✓ b. That's a tough one. I'd say it's probably always being in the public eye. You have no privacy.

c. Good question. Actually, I can't imagine doing anything else, really.

d. It's hard to say. There are so many good actors. I admire a lot of them.

e. Oh, definitely. I try to set a good example for young people.

4 To be famous or not to be famous . . .

Conversation strategies | **Number the lines of the conversation in the correct order.**

_____ But if you were famous, you would be hanging out with other famous people, wouldn't you? That sounds like fun to me!

_____ It's hard to say. Even if you're famous, you might not make a lot of money. Some politicians are famous, but they aren't rich – and they don't wear expensive clothes!

_1_ You want to be an actor, right? You *would* like to be famous someday, wouldn't you?

_____ I'm not saying that wouldn't be fun. I just kind of like my privacy, that's all.

_____ Oh, that's a tough question. Being famous would be nice, but I don't know if I'd like all the stuff that goes with it. I like acting. But that doesn't mean I want to be famous!

_____ I know what you mean, but just think, you'd make a lot of money. Then you could buy all kinds of cool clothes, couldn't you?

1 Rap image

Reading | **A Read the article. Why do you think rap stars maintain their "bad boy" image?**

From Rap to Riches

From RAP to Riches

While rap music is now a mainstream part of the music industry, it began in the 1970s in a poor part of New York City, where life was often difficult and dangerous because of crime, unemployment, and violence. At that time, rappers like Grandmaster Flash and the Furious Five created rap as a form of poetry that reflected the way people like themselves lived in hard, inner-city neighborhoods. Soon, hanging out with friends and rapping became a way for many teenagers living on such tough city streets to express themselves creatively. Rap quickly spread to other cities in the United States and then became a worldwide phenomenon.

Even after its global success, many rap stars, such as 50 Cent, Jay Z, Lil Wayne, Nicki Minaj, and Wiz Khalifa, still come from poor urban neighborhoods. Moreover, as rap artists become rich and famous,

many choose to keep their tough "street image." Their songs continue to reflect the language of the neighborhoods where they grew up, and their clothes and accessories reflect – and influence – the style of urban youth around the world. However, some music fans are uncomfortable with the "bad boy" image of rap, and are critical especially of gangsta rappers, who often include violent lyrics in their songs.

Rap is now part of a larger cultural phenomenon known as hip-hop, which has become a successful and profitable industry. Hip-hop has influenced movies like *Hustle & Flow*, which follows an aspiring musician from his disadvantaged youth through his eventual success. It has also influenced fashion design, such as Sean John (Sean Combs' fashion line) and G-Unit (50 Cent's fashion line). Even professional sports teams are influenced by rap stars – Jay Z is now a part owner of the Brooklyn Nets, an NBA basketball team in New York City.

It's hard to imagine that rap stars haven't always been rich, famous, and influential, or that their early lives may have been difficult or even tragic. However, with some luck, a lot of hard work, and talent, rappers have entered the mainstream, providing not only entertainment, but reminding us of the tough environment that created it.

Jay Z

Nicki Minaj

B Read the article again. Write *T* (true) or *F* (false). Then correct the false statements.

1. Rap started in a ~~wealthy~~ *poor* neighborhood in New York City in the 1970s. _F_

2. Rap was a way for kids in bad neighborhoods to travel to other cities. _____

3. After rap became popular, many of its stars came from rich backgrounds. _____

4. 50 Cent came from a privileged background. _____

5. Rap music is often criticized for its violence. _____

6. Rap and hip-hop have inspired movies and clothing. _____

2 A controversial rap star

Writing **A** Read the paragraph about Eminem. Underline the topic sentence. Then cross out any information that does not support the topic.

Eminem is one of the most popular and controversial rap stars of all time. He is known for his distinctive style of changing his pace several times within a song without losing the beat. He often uses a lot of bad language in his songs. He has been married and has three children. He is also famous for telling stories in his songs, talking about his own life and childhood, making fun of celebrities, and criticizing politicians. He has short blond hair, and often wears baggy jeans and sweatshirts. Unlike most rap stars who come from New York and Los Angeles, Eminem is from Detroit.

B Write a paragraph about a famous person. Write a strong topic sentence, and add more information and details in supporting sentences.

Unit 10 Progress chart

What can you do? Mark the boxes. ☑ = I can . . .　　　　　❓ = I need to review how to . . .	To review, go back to these pages in the Student's Book.
Grammar	
☐ talk hypothetically about the past using *if* clauses with the past perfect form of the verb and past modals.	98 and 99
☐ use negative and affirmative tag questions.	100 and 101
Vocabulary	
☐ use at least 8 idiomatic expressions to talk about fame.	98, 99, 100, and 101
Conversation strategies	
☐ soften advice and give encouragement using tag questions.	102
☐ use expressions like *It's hard to say* when questions are difficult to answer.	103
Writing	
☐ write a paragraph with a topic sentence and supporting sentences.	105

1 On the web

Vocabulary Complete the questions with the words in the box.

financial support	outsource	shortage	unemployment
obsessed	recruit	traffic congestion	✓ wireless Internet access

---

Search — The Internet Search Engine

Images Groups News Local More>>

[SEARCH]

Web   Results of **1-100** of about **969,000** for **Washingtonville** *(0.30 seconds)*

Results for current top news stories: Local: Washingtonville

Technology news

A local coffee shop is offering free _wireless Internet access_ . The owner says it's necessary to compete with the large coffee shop chains.

Business

Several companies have announced they will _____ their customer service jobs and lay off staff. Local _____ rates are expected to jump 3%.

Increased demand for the latest hybrid cars has created a _____ at local car dealers.

Local companies are expecting to _____ over 600 employees at the annual job fair this year.

Health

Is our culture _____ with dieting and being thin? Dr. Murphy examines the diet craze and the new "designer" diets.

Education

Tuition fees at colleges across the country are rising at an alarming rate. Local financial expert Ken Rose explains what kind of _____ is available.

Local traffic

_____ is expected in the Washingtonville Bridge area again tomorrow. Delays are due to the ongoing bridge repairs.

Page 1 ◁ ▷

2 Current trends

Grammar | Complete the sentences with the passive form of the present continuous or present perfect. Sometimes there is more than one correct answer.

1. Technology companies have developed a tablet with a much tougher screen glass. These tablets _are being sold_ (sell) in stores and online right now.

2. Major airlines have now bought a new type of airplane which _____ (develop) to lower fuel consumption.

3. Scientists are exploring ways to make plants like wheat, corn, and tomatoes disease-resistant. These plants _____ (engineer) and tested on farms around the world.

4. Sports clothing companies are trying to incorporate technology into their clothing. Currently, vests, shirts, and pants _____ (create) to help athletes improve their performance by measuring muscle activity.

5. Many companies have now outsourced information technology jobs. These jobs _____ (move) overseas to cut company costs.

6. Research has shown that children in the United States are gaining weight. Several studies _____ (conduct) by researchers and show that 30% of U.S. children are overweight.

3 In the news

Grammar | Write sentences about the headlines using the verbs given. Use the passive form of the present continuous or the present perfect. Sometimes more than one answer is possible.

> **At last, a cure for the common cold**

1. (find) _At last, a cure for the common cold has been found._

> **The world's oldest building in Japan**

2. (discover) _____

> **New driving tests for next year**

3. (schedule) _____

> **Traffic slow because of strong storms**

4. (delay) _____

> **Plans to hire more teachers**

5. (discuss) _____

1 An environmental puzzle

Vocabulary | Complete the sentences. Then write the highlighted letters in order to complete the sentence below.

1. Many fish are dying because of the _t_ _o_ _x_ _i_ _c_
   _c_ _h_ _e_ _m_ _i_ _c_ _a_ _l_ _s_ that factories dump into rivers every day.

2. Scientists think that polar ice caps are melting at an ever-increasing rate
   because of ____ ____ ____ ____ ____ ____ ____ ____ ____ ____ .

3. Garbage that isn't recycled ends up in a ____ ____ ____ ____ ____ ____ ____ .

4. If we continue to use our ____ ____ ____ ____ ____ ____
   ____ ____ ____ ____ ____ ____ ____ ____ , like oil and coal, they might run out.

5. I want a car that ____ ____ ____ ____ ____ ____ less gas because
   gas prices are rising!

6. Due to the lack of rain, we are experiencing a ____ ____ ____ ____ ____ ____ .

7. Scientists have been working on ____ ____ ____ ____ ____ ____
   ____ ____ ____ ____ ____ ____ ____ ____ ____ ____ ____ ____
   transportation, like electric cars, to cut down on pollution.

8. Some synthetic materials are not ____ ____ ____ ____ ____ ____ ____ ____
   ____ ____ ____ ____ .

_____ energy by turning off lights when you leave home.

2 Conservation tips

Vocabulary | Circle the correct words to complete the sentences. Then check (✓) the things you do to help.

1. ____ Use **biodegradable** / (**energy-saving**)/ **global warming** home appliances to cut back on electricity use.

2. ____ Avoid using plastic containers that take years to **consume** / **recycle** / **decompose** in landfill sites.

3. ____ Encourage government officials to pass tougher laws to reduce **air pollution** / **public transportation** / **endangered species**.

4. ____ Take shorter showers and remember to turn off the faucet while you brush your teeth to reduce **nuclear waste** / **water consumption** / **water pollution**.

5. ____ Try to **recycle** / **consume** / **use** plastic, paper, and glass if possible.

6. ____ Buy appliances like refrigerators and air conditioners that **lack** / **decompose** / **consume** lower amounts of energy.

7. ____ Be aware of companies that **protect** / **contaminate** / **conserve** rivers with toxic chemicals, and don't buy their products.

8. ____ If you think you **buy** / **take** / **lack** information on ways to save energy or conserve water, search the Internet for ideas.

Environmental awareness

Grammar | Circle the word or expression that best fits each sentence.

1. I think the majority of people would prefer to buy organic produce **due to** / **despite** the high cost.

2. We always turn our heat down a few degrees in the winter **in order to** / **instead of** save money on oil.

3. Gas prices have gone up **due to** / **although** oil shortages.

4. We try to recycle plastic, paper, and glass, **although** / **so that** it's sometimes hard to do.

5. We're experiencing more hurricanes and severe storms **as a result of** / **because** global warming.

6. I think some people aren't very aware of environmental problems **instead of** / **because of** a lack of education.

It's important because . . .

Grammar | Complete the sentences with the words and expressions in the box.

> ✓because   due to   in order to   in spite of   instead of   so that

1. It's important to keep the world's oceans and seas free of pollution and contamination ____*because*____ we depend on these waters for food.

2. Car companies are beginning to make some cars out of lightweight carbon fiber instead of steel _____ increase gas mileage.

3. Governments need to work together _____ endangered species are protected around the world.

4. Some rain forests are being deforested twice as quickly as previously thought _____ logging activities.

5. Governments should invest in renewable energy _____ the cost.

6. Some people use vegetable oil to run their cars _____ gasoline.

About you

Grammar and vocabulary | Complete the sentences with true information. Use linking words and expressions.

1. I try to use _less electricity in order to save money each month_____.

2. I try not to waste _____.

3. I always buy _____.

4. I'm concerned about _____.

5. I'm not concerned about _____.

6. I think governments should _____.

1 Referring back

Conversation
strategies
A Taya and Yasuo are talking about current trends. Match Taya's comments with Yasuo's comments later in the conversation.

1. A lot of big companies are employing workers like computer programmers overseas because it's cheaper. I'm not sure that's fair. __e__

2. I think we have some of the longest working hours in the world in this country. It's awful. _____

3. The cost of a college education is so expensive. It's not fair that students have thousands of dollars of debt when they graduate. _____

4. I think it's great that people can work more from home now. It's much better for family life. _____

5. I heard they're increasing the retirement age to 70! I mean, do you think people should work that long? _____

a. Like you were saying, not commuting every day can only be good for everyone, especially people with kids.

b. As you said, it's not right that students have to start their careers owing so much money in student loans.

c. Going back to what you were saying about raising the retirement age, I actually think it's a good idea.

d. Like you said earlier, it's not good to do so much overtime. How do people spend time with their families?

e. You mentioned transferring jobs abroad earlier. I agree that it's not good for local workers.

B Look at Taya's comments in part A again. Refer back to each comment she makes and add your own view.

1. _As Taya was saying, I don't think big companies should move jobs overseas._
   I mean, what will people do here to earn money?

2. _____

3. _____

4. _____

5. _____

2 And so on and so forth . . .

Conversation
strategies | Complete the conversations with the phrases in the box and more formal
vague expressions like *and so forth*, *and so on*, or *etc.*

✓chemical engineers, electrical engineers, more on-the-job experience, good leadership qualities, organizational skills, good people skills,	paid leave, flexible work hours, relax, reduce stress, pursue interests, vision care, dental care,

1. A I think engineering is a great field for students to study. It offers some of the best-paid jobs for students just graduating from college.

    B Yes. Some of the highest starting salaries go to *chemical engineers, electrical engineers, etc.*

2. A It's too bad that some companies are cutting back on medical benefits.

    B Yeah, I know. My company has cut things like _____.

3. A I don't think it's fair that companies are encouraging older workers to retire because they make more money than younger workers.

    B I totally agree. Older workers have _____.

4. A I'm thinking about starting a family, but I'm really nervous about trying to work and raise a child at the same time.

    B I wouldn't worry. Lots of companies offer new parents benefits like _____.

5. A I think when you're hiring a new employee, you need someone with a good personality. I think personality is the most important thing.

    B I agree, but I also think you should look for someone with _____.

6. A I think all workers should have at least four weeks of paid vacation a year.

    B Absolutely. I mean, vacations allow people to _____.

3 About you

Conversation
strategies | Imagine you heard these comments in a conversation. Refer back to them
and give your view. Use a formal vague expession.

1. "There should be fines for people who don't recycle."
    As you said, fines would make people recycle, make money to improve recycling programs, and so on.

2. "Global warming is really impacting our climate."
    _____

3. "People should use public transportation."
    _____

1 Trendy words

Reading | **Match the terms with the definitions. Read the article to check your answers.**

1. cyberchondriacs __e__

2. e-quaintances _____

3. phishers _____

4. wikis _____

5. MOOCs _____

6. selfies _____

a. friends who meet through social websites, but may not be friends in real life

b. people who attempt to steal other people's identities

c. pictures people take of themselves to upload to a social network / networking website

d. web pages that anyone can add to and / or change

✓e. people who are convinced they are sick because of medical information they found online

f. online classes offered by colleges that anyone can attend for free

---

Internet Vocabulary

Dozens of new words enter the language every year. Many of these have emerged to reflect advances in technology and the ways we use it. Some may stick, and others may fall out of use or change their meaning over time. Here are a number of recent additions. How long will they be around with their current meaning? Only time will tell.

cyberchondriac   A cyberchondriac visits health and medical websites to read about the symptoms of different diseases, illnesses, or medical conditions. Then, like any hypochondriac, the cyberchondriac becomes worried, thinking he or she has the particular symptoms he or she just read about.

e-quaintance   An e-quaintance is a person who you communicate with exclusively through online interactions like instant messaging at work or Internet dating – an online acquaintance. An e-quaintance might be a person you email for help with computer issues at work or a person who has similar interests as you do on gaming websites.

phishing   Phishing describes the Internet crime of trying to get someone's personal information (bank account numbers, national identification numbers, etc.) by sending official-looking emails and directing unsuspecting victims to fake websites. When the victim supplies the updated information to these fake websites, the phisher uses the information to take money from the person's bank account, run up credit card debts, or take out loans in his or her name.

wiki   A website where users can add or modify text is called a *wiki*. Wikis differ from blogs in that any user can visit a wiki page to search for or update information, making it a continuous work in progress.

MOOC   MOOC is an acronym for Massive Open Online Course, a type of course given by colleges and universities around the world. A MOOC is a class open to anyone who wants to follow along on the Internet. For instance, a student in Japan can enroll in a physics course taught by a professor at an American college through a MOOC for no cost. MOOCs are being made available more and more as online learning has become more popular.

selfie   A selfie is a picture that a social networking user takes of him- or herself to post on a profile page. A selfie is usually taken at arm's length and sometimes involves a funny face or gesture. Selfies aren't just being taken by teenagers, they're also taken by celebrities, parents, and even grandparents!

2 Trend watch

Writing **A** Use the words and expressions in the box to complete the blog entry.

declined   fewer   growing   increasingly   less   ✓more and more

Blog

Have you noticed that _more and more_ people use their phones for everything? I mean, everywhere you go, you just see people using their phones. Even my grandparents take videos of us with their phones. They never bring their video cameras anymore. It just seems that _____ people are using them these days. I bet the sales of video cameras and things have _____ due to smartphones. I mean, it's just _____ common to use your phone for everything these days. When I go away for the weekend, I don't even take my computer anymore. It's _____ trouble to just take my phone and use that for email and everything. I use it instead of my credit card too now – like the number of stores that let you pay by phone is _____ . So it's really convenient.

B Write a blog entry about a trend you've noticed in your town or city. Use words and expressions from part A.

Blog

Unit 11 Progress chart

What can you do? Mark the boxes. ✓ = I can . . .　　　? = I need to review how to . . .	To review, go back to these pages in the Student's Book.
Grammar — use the passive of the present continuous and present perfect. link ideas with expressions like *although*, *due to*, and *so that*.	108 and 109 110 and 111
Vocabulary — use at least 8 new expressions to describe trends in society. use at least 15 new expressions to discuss the environment.	108 and 109 110 and 111
Conversation strategies — refer back to what someone said with expressions like *As you were saying*, *Like you said*, etc. use formal vague expressions like *and so forth* and *etc.*	112 113
Writing — use expressions like *increasingly* to describe trends.	115

89

Careers

Lesson A | Finding a career

1 Words for job success

Vocabulary | Complete the definitions.

1. The document that lists your educational history and work experience is your _resumé_ .

2. If you work for a company for a short time to get some work experience, it's called an _____ .

3. Someone who can give you guidance and help you choose the right job is a _____ _____ .

4. A meeting where you are asked about your qualifications by a potential employer is an _____ .

5. The things you are good at are your _____ , and the things you are not good at are your _____ .

6. A questionnaire that helps you see what kind of person you are is a _____ _____ .

2 What you need to do is take my advice!

Grammar | Fern is having some problems at work. Read her concerns and then use the cues to give her advice. Use *What* clauses.

1. **Fern** I don't feel my boss notices me. I wonder how I can make her see that I'm ready to take on more responsibility and get promoted.

   You _What you need is a positive attitude._
   (You need a positive attitude.)

   You _____
   (My friend did something really smart. She wrote a letter to her boss.)

2. **Fern** I've been working here for over a year. How can I ask my boss for a raise?

   You _____
   (I would just ask.)

   You _____
   (You need to get another job offer and then ask for a promotion.)

3. **Fern** I don't think my colleagues take me seriously. How do I get more respect?

   You _____
   (You should wear formal business clothes.)

   You _____
   (You need to get additional skills.)

3 The job market

Grammar | Rewrite the advice below starting with the long noun phrase given.

1. Try and get a really good degree.

   The first thing to do _is to try and get a really good degree_____.

2. Get some work experience in a successful company.

   One good thing to get _____.

3. Be determined to succeed.

   The main thing you need to be _____.

4. Companies are hiring new graduates right now.

   The good news _____.

5. Work on improving your English.

   The best thing to do _____.

6. Internships help you get better jobs.

   The good thing about internships _____.

4 Online advice

Grammar | Write two answers for the job seekers' online message board. Start one with a *What* clause and another with a long noun phrase.

Message Board

JOB-SEEKING ADVICE

QUESTION: I had planned to work for a law office during my summer break, but they just told me that they don't need me. I need a summer job fast! What can I do?

Answer: 1. _What I would do is ask your friends and family members if they_
have any temporary jobs available in their companies.

2. _____
_____

QUESTION: I would love to work at a ski resort for the winter. Does anyone have any ideas about what I could do, and how I can get a job?

Answer: 3. _____
_____

4. _____
_____

QUESTION: I don't know what I want to do with my life. Any suggestions for a recent college graduate who hates to get up in the morning?

Answer: 5. _____
_____

6. _____
_____

---

1 What's the job?

Vocabulary | Complete the jobs with the vowels *a, e, i, o,* or *u.* Then match them to the areas of work they belong to. Write *A, B, C,* or *D.*

A = Construction industry
B = Financial services

C = Media and communications
D = Medicine and health care

1. e d i t o r   _C_
2. s __ r g __ __ n   ____
3. s t __ c k b r __ k __ r   ____
4. c __ n t r __ c t __ r   ____
5. w r __ t __ r   ____
6. p __ d __ __ t r __ c __ __ n   ____

7. t __ x __ d v __ s __ r   ____
8. c __ n s t r __ c t __ __ n w __ r k __ r   ____
9. p s y c h __ __ t r __ c n __ r s __   ____
10. __ n t __ r p r __ t __ r   ____
11. f __ n __ n c __ __ __ l __ n __ l y s t   ____
12. t r __ n s l __ t __ r   ____

2 What jobs are you suited for?

Vocabulary | Read what each person says about himself or herself. Write one area of work that each person is suited for and one area of work that each person isn't suited for.

advertising	✓finance	public relations	the travel industry
business management	journalism	publishing	
the construction industry	✓medicine	telemarketing	

1. My parents wanted me to be a doctor, but I can't stand the sight of blood. What I enjoy most is anything to do with money, like banking and investments.

   Suited for: _____*finance*_____   Not suited for: _____*medicine*_____

2. I love words, and I'm a pretty good writer. My friends often ask me to look over their papers for mistakes, and I enjoy that. I don't want a job with too much responsibility, like being involved in the planning or organization of a company.

   Suited for: _____   Not suited for: _____

3. I really enjoy building things. In fact, I helped my dad design and build a barn for our farm last year. I'm not really good at things like reading and writing. I'm more practical. Like, I can't imagine writing articles for a newspaper, for example.

   Suited for: _____   Not suited for: _____

4. I'm very sociable and love going to parties and events. I really like meeting people, and I think I'm a good communicator – I get along well with everyone. I would hate being in an office all day and talking to people on the phone.

   Suited for: _____   Not suited for: _____

5. I'm a homebody, so I don't want a job that takes me away from home a lot. One thing that interests me is how companies promote their products to customers.

   Suited for: _____   Not suited for: _____

3 What's in your future?

Grammar Complete the conversations with the future continuous or the future perfect.
Sometimes you can use *may (not)* and *might (not)* instead of *will* or *won't*.

1. **Sasha** I have no idea what I want to do when I graduate from
   college next year. I really need to make a decision soon!

   Tia Oh, two years from now, you *might / will be running*
   (run) your own business.

   Sasha No, I _____ probably _____ (look) for
   a job that pays more than $7 an hour. But hopefully, I
   _____ (not ask) you to lend me money!

   Tia That'll be great! But seriously, two years from now, you
   _____ (finish) your degree, and you
   _____ (work) on Wall Street.

   Sasha Hmm . . . maybe, or I _____ (live) on a Caribbean
   island and _____ (work) on the beach.

2. **Malik** I can't believe another year has gone by already.

   Jamie I know. It goes by so fast. I wonder what we
   _____ (do) this time next year.

   Malik Oh, I don't know. We _____ (live) someplace
   else, and we _____ (take) a luxury vacation!

   Jamie Yeah, right. We _____ (not pay off) our debts by
   then, and we still _____ (not fix up) this house, and . . .

   Malik Oh, I hope we _____ (finish) it all by then.

4 About you

Grammar Answer the questions with true information. Use the future continuous and future perfect.

1. What do you think your life will be like ten years from now?
   I think I'll be working in another country and making a lot of money!

2. Will you still be taking English classes?
   _____

3. What job do you think you'll be doing?
   _____

4. Do you think you'll have changed jobs more than once?
   _____

5. Where will you be living?
   _____

6. Do you think you'll have gotten married or had children?
   _____

1 The reason I ask is . . .

Complete the conversations with the noun phrases and *What* clauses in the box.

the best thing was (that)	what I heard was (that)
✓ the reason I ask is (that)	what I thought was good was (that)
the worst part was (that)	what I was going to tell you was (that)

1. **Jamal** Didn't you once get a job on a farm in Australia?

   Ryan Yeah, I did. Why?

   Jamal Well, *the reason I ask is* _____ I was wondering whether I should try that myself.

   Ryan You know, I picked garlic. It was hard work, and _____ I smelled like garlic every day. I had to take a long shower at the end of the day to get rid of the garlic smell.

   Jamal Hmm. I think I'd prefer to work on a fruit farm.

2. **Ming-li** Did you hear that the department store at the mall is hiring?

   Thalia No, I didn't. Do you know what positions they're hiring for?

   Ming-li Well, _____ they're hiring temporary sales help for the holiday season. I think the jobs last through the middle of January.

   Thalia Sounds good. I'd love to make a little extra money during the school break. I'll check it out next week.

   Ming-li You should probably go sooner than next week. _____ the store is only hiring about ten people.

   Thalia Ooh. You're right. I'll go today!

3. **Tomo** What did you think about the job interview we had with Andy Fowler?

   Celia Well, I kind of liked him. _____ he had some really interesting ideas about promoting our products. I think he'd be successful in our advertising department.

   Tomo Yeah, he seemed good. He had great qualifications, he'd done his research, and _____ he has a positive attitude. He doesn't have much solid experience, though.

   Celia Well, you need to be hired to get experience. Maybe we should give him a chance.

2 I don't know if you saw . . .

Conversation strategies | Read the advertisements. Write sentences about the advertisements with *I don't know if* . . . and the cues.

> **WANTED: Energetic, friendly waiters and waitresses to work evenings. Call Sergio at the Cactus Bistro for an interview at 888–555–9609.**

1. (see / hire) *I don't know if you've seen the advertisement, but they're hiring waiters and waitresses at the Cactus Bistro.*

> Interested in a new job? Visit the Johnstown Technical College job fair this weekend. Local companies want to meet graduates in business management and information technology.

2. (look for / have) _____

> Need help writing or revising your résumé? Get creative writing ideas from Résumé Express. Call us today at 888-555-4265.

3. (think about rewriting / get help) _____

> **Announcement**: Lakewood University is now offering a business management degree with an emphasis on advertising and public relations. We are currently taking applications for the fall semester.

4. (hear / get a degree) _____

3 I need some help.

Conversation strategies | Number the lines of the conversation in the correct order.

_____ Maybe you should get some advice somewhere. I don't know if you're familiar with the Job Resource Center, but they can give you tips on how to interview better.

_____ Really? I didn't know you had help finding your job.

_____ I think I *have* heard of it. Is it on Maple Street, near the park?

_____ Oh, yeah. I never would have gotten the job I have right now without their help. The best part was that they gave me a lot of help with things like writing my résumé and improving my interview skills.

_1_ I've interviewed for six jobs in the past couple of weeks, and I still haven't been hired. I really need some help.

_____ Well, I really need to get a job soon, so I'd better check out the Job Resource Center today!

_____ Yeah, it is. When I was looking for a job last year, I met with a career counselor there.

1 After a job interview

Reading | **A Read the article. Then add the correct heading to each section.**

Use the Information Highway   What's the Plan?   It Pays to Be Polite

Following Up After a Job Interview

Congratulations! You were contacted to interview for an amazing job – your dream job – and it went really well. The interviewer was encouraging and easy to talk to. The job location is convenient, and the salary is more than you make now! You're beyond happy! However, it's been almost two weeks since the interview, and you haven't heard from the interviewer or a company representative. Why aren't they calling you? And what should you do?

Many job seekers worry about contacting an interviewer after an interview – even people who feel they made a positive impression. However, contacting the interviewer after the interview is the best thing you can do! Following are three polite and professional ways to remind an interviewer why you are the ideal candidate for a job.

_____

Before finishing up an interview, remember to ask the interviewer what the next steps are in the process – this will give you an idea of the interviewer's timetable, and it will give you a time frame for following up if you need to. If the interviewer tells you it will take about two weeks before he or she makes a final decision, it's perfectly appropriate to contact him or her a few days after that deadline has passed with a short, polite note asking if a decision has been reached.

_____

Always, always, always write a thank-you note after an interview – as soon as you can. The main reason for following up is that it keeps you fresh in the interviewer's mind, and shows that you are professional and well organized, as well as appreciative. Employers like that. Further, it gives you an opportunity to restate your interest in the position and remind the interviewer why you are a great choice. But keep it brief!

_____

Finally, try to look upon the interview process as a way of making professional connections. Make sure you are signed up to work-related networking sites and ask the interviewer if you can connect with him or her. Even if you don't get hired for this job, you still have a way to communicate with professionals in the field you want to work in. Who knows, maybe another job will open up at the company and the interviewer will think of you!

B Read the article again. Which statements are true? Which are false? Write _T_ or _F_.

1. Waiting for the company to contact you after an interview is the only thing to do. _____

2. One thing you should do at an interview is ask what the next steps are. _____

3. Interviewers like thank-you notes because they show your appreciation. _____

4. Thank-you notes give you a chance to put in writing everything you said at the interview. _____

5. It's appropriate to contact an interviewer on a networking site before an interview. _____

6. An interview for a job you don't get can sometimes lead to other opportunities. _____

2 Please consider me.

Writing | **A** Read the cover letter. Then complete it with the expressions in the box.

advertised on October 28	cover letter	Sincerely
attached résumé	Dear	Thank you for your time and consideration.

Application Form

Application for: **JUNIOR BAKER**

Upload a résumé

Include a (1) _____

Submit

(2) _____ Sir or Madam,

I am applying for the position of Junior Baker, which was (3) _____ . I am currently a third-year student at the Oakland School of Culinary Arts, and baking is my passion.

As you can see from the (4) _____ , I don't have a lot of experience in commercial baking. I had a part-time job in my school's cafeteria. I was responsible for baking bread and rolls for over 200 students and faculty members every weekend. I am a diligent worker, and I think I would be an asset to your company.

I would welcome the chance to speak with you at your convenience. I can be reached at 888-555-2387 from 8 a.m. to 1 p.m. every day.

(5) _____

(6) _____ ,

Melvin Cruz

B Write a cover letter to apply for a job you'd really like to have. Include an opening paragraph, middle paragraph, closing paragraph, and ending.

Unit 12 Progress chart

What can you do? Mark the boxes. ✓ = I can . . . ? = I need to review how to . . .	To review, go back to these pages in the Student's Book.
Grammar ▸ ☐ use *What* clauses and long noun phrases as subjects.	118 and 119
☐ talk about the future with the future continuous and future perfect.	120 and 121
Vocabulary ▸ ☐ use at least 20 new words to talk about careers.	120 and 121
Conversation strategies ▸ ☐ introduce what I say with expressions like *What I read was*	122
☐ introduce ideas with *I don't know if*	123
Writing ▸ ☐ write a cover letter.	125

Illustration credits

Chuck Gonzales: 2, 3, 20, 21, 31, 44, 45, 54, 55, 94   **Frank Montagna:** 10, 11, 26, 27, 46, 47, 52, 67, 76, 78, 79   **Marilena Perilli:** 6, 7, 22, 23, 40, 58, 70, 71, 93   **Greg White:** 18, 38, 61, 69   **Terry Wong:** 12, 13, 28, 29, 50, 62, 63, 83, 90   **Q2A Studio Artists:** 59, 72

Photo credits

4 *(top to bottom)* ©Polka Dot Images/Thinkstock; ©Punchstock; ©Ryan McVay/Thinkstock   **5** ©newphotoservice/Shutterstock
8 ©RON EDMONDS/Associated Press   **14** ©Getty Images   **15** ©Punchstock   **16** *(left to right)* ©Mel Curtis/Getty Images/RF;
©Tim Garcha/Corbis; ©Kaz Chiba/Getty Images   **18** © Tongro Image Stock/agefotostoc   **19** *(top to bottom)* ©Tim Thompson/Corbis;
©David Lyons/Alamy; ©Watt, Elizabeth/agefotostock *(background)* ©Malchev/Shutterstock   **24** ©Jim Arbogast/Getty Images/RF
30 ©Zero Creatives/Getty Images   **31** ©Westend61/Getty Images/RF   **32** ©Ryan McVay/Thinkstock   **34** ©Punchstock
42 ©SnowWhiteimages/Shutterstock   **49** ©Sean Gladwell/Shutterstock   **60** *(top to bottom)* ©Andresr/Shutterstock; ©arek_malang/
Shutterstock; © Ocean/Corbis/RF; © photomak/Shutterstock   **64** ©ColinCramm/Shutterstock   **66** ©SuperStock/agefotostock
67 ©George Doyle/Thinkstock   **72** *(books)* ©LanKS/Shutterstock   **74** *(top to bottom)* ©Kevork Djansezian/Getty Images; ©Thinkstock/
Getty Images; ©PhotoAlto/James Hardy   **75** *(top to bottom)* ©Kike Calvo/National Geographic Society/Corbis; ©Lane Oatey/Blue Jean
Images/Getty Images/RF; ©Digital Vision/Getty Images; ©Punchstock; ©Wayne Eardley/Masterfile   **77** *(top, top to bottom)* ©s_bukley/
Shutterstock; ©Helga Esteb/Shutterstock *(bottom, left to right)* ©MGM/courtesy Everett Collection; ©MGM/courtesy Everett Collection;
©20th Century Fox Film Corp/Everett Collection; ©Alexandra Wyman/Getty Images   **80** *(left to right)* © D Dipasupil/FilmMagic/Getty
Images; ©Jason LaVeris/FilmMagic/Getty Images *(diamond)* ©pdesign/Shutterstock *(background)* ©Ezepov Dmitry/Shutterstock
85 ©Sue Wilson/Alamy   **86** ©Randy Faris/Corbis

Text credits

While every effort has been made, it has not always been possible to identify the sources of all the material
used, or to trace all copyright holders. If any omissions are brought to our notice, we will be happy to include
the appropriate acknowledgements on reprinting.

The top 500 spoken words

This is a list of the top 500 words in spoken North American English. It is based on a sample of four and a half million words of conversation from the Cambridge International Corpus. The most frequent word, *I*, is at the top of the list.

1. I	40. really	79. see
2. and	41. with	80. how
3. the	42. he	81. they're
4. you	43. one	82. kind
5. uh	44. are	83. here
6. to	45. this	84. from
7. a	46. there	85. did
8. that	47. I'm	86. something
9. it	48. all	87. too
10. of	49. if	88. more
11. yeah	50. no	89. very
12. know	51. get	90. want
13. in	52. about	91. little
14. like	53. at	92. been
15. they	54. out	93. things
16. have	55. had	94. an
17. so	56. then	95. you're
18. was	57. because	96. said
19. but	58. go	97. there's
20. is	59. up	98. I've
21. it's	60. she	99. much
22. we	61. when	100. where
23. huh	62. them	101. two
24. just	63. can	102. thing
25. oh	64. would	103. her
26. do	65. as	104. didn't
27. don't	66. me	105. other
28. that's	67. mean	106. say
29. well	68. some	107. back
30. for	69. good	108. could
31. what	70. got	109. their
32. on	71. OK	110. our
33. think	72. people	111. guess
34. right	73. now	112. yes
35. not	74. going	113. way
36. um	75. were	114. has
37. or	76. lot	115. down
38. my	77. your	116. we're
39. be	78. time	117. any

The top 500 spoken words

118. he's	161. five	204. sort
119. work	162. always	205. great
120. take	163. school	206. bad
121. even	164. look	207. we've
122. those	165. still	208. another
123. over	166. around	209. car
124. probably	167. anything	210. true
125. him	168. kids	211. whole
126. who	169. first	212. whatever
127. put	170. does	213. twenty
128. years	171. need	214. after
129. sure	172. us	215. ever
130. can't	173. should	216. find
131. pretty	174. talking	217. care
132. gonna	175. last	218. better
133. stuff	176. thought	219. hard
134. come	177. doesn't	220. haven't
135. these	178. different	221. trying
136. by	179. money	222. give
137. into	180. long	223. I'd
138. went	181. used	224. problem
139. make	182. getting	225. else
140. than	183. same	226. remember
141. year	184. four	227. might
142. three	185. every	228. again
143. which	186. new	229. pay
144. home	187. everything	230. try
145. will	188. many	231. place
146. nice	189. before	232. part
147. never	190. though	233. let
148. only	191. most	234. keep
149. his	192. tell	235. children
150. doing	193. being	236. anyway
151. cause	194. bit	237. came
152. off	195. house	238. six
153. I'll	196. also	239. family
154. maybe	197. use	240. wasn't
155. real	198. through	241. talk
156. why	199. feel	242. made
157. big	200. course	243. hundred
158. actually	201. what's	244. night
159. she's	202. old	245. call
160. day	203. done	246. saying

The top 500 spoken words

247. dollars	290. started	333. believe
248. live	291. job	334. thinking
249. away	292. says	335. funny
250. either	293. play	336. state
251. read	294. usually	337. until
252. having	295. wow	338. husband
253. far	296. exactly	339. idea
254. watch	297. took	340. name
255. week	298. few	341. seven
256. mhm	299. child	342. together
257. quite	300. thirty	343. each
258. enough	301. buy	344. hear
259. next	302. person	345. help
260. couple	303. working	346. nothing
261. own	304. half	347. parents
262. wouldn't	305. looking	348. room
263. ten	306. someone	349. today
264. interesting	307. coming	350. makes
265. am	308. eight	351. stay
266. sometimes	309. love	352. mom
267. bye	310. everybody	353. sounds
268. seems	311. able	354. change
269. heard	312. we'll	355. understand
270. goes	313. life	356. such
271. called	314. may	357. gone
272. point	315. both	358. system
273. ago	316. type	359. comes
274. while	317. end	360. thank
275. fact	318. least	361. show
276. once	319. told	362. thousand
277. seen	320. saw	363. left
278. wanted	321. college	364. friends
279. isn't	322. ones	365. class
280. start	323. almost	366. already
281. high	324. since	367. eat
282. somebody	325. days	368. small
283. let's	326. couldn't	369. boy
284. times	327. gets	370. paper
285. guy	328. guys	371. world
286. area	329. god	372. best
287. fun	330. country	373. water
288. they've	331. wait	374. myself
289. you've	332. yet	375. run

The top 500 spoken words

376. they'll	418. company	460. sorry
377. won't	419. friend	461. living
378. movie	420. set	462. drive
379. cool	421. minutes	463. outside
380. news	422. morning	464. bring
381. number	423. between	465. easy
382. man	424. music	466. stop
383. basically	425. close	467. percent
384. nine	426. leave	468. hand
385. enjoy	427. wife	469. gosh
386. bought	428. knew	470. top
387. whether	429. pick	471. cut
388. especially	430. important	472. computer
389. taking	431. ask	473. tried
390. sit	432. hour	474. gotten
391. book	433. deal	475. mind
392. fifty	434. mine	476. business
393. months	435. reason	477. anybody
394. women	436. credit	478. takes
395. month	437. dog	479. aren't
396. found	438. group	480. question
397. side	439. turn	481. rather
398. food	440. making	482. twelve
399. looks	441. American	483. phone
400. summer	442. weeks	484. program
401. hmm	443. certain	485. without
402. fine	444. less	486. moved
403. hey	445. must	487. gave
404. student	446. dad	488. yep
405. agree	447. during	489. case
406. mother	448. lived	490. looked
407. problems	449. forty	491. certainly
408. city	450. air	492. talked
409. second	451. government	493. beautiful
410. definitely	452. eighty	494. card
411. spend	453. wonderful	495. walk
412. happened	454. seem	496. married
413. hours	455. wrong	497. anymore
414. war	456. young	498. you'll
415. matter	457. places	499. middle
416. supposed	458. girl	500. tax
417. worked	459. happen	